TIL ALL THE STARS HAVE FALLEN

Canadian Poems For Children

Selected by
David Booth

Illustrated by
Kady MacDonald Denton

Kids Can Press Ltd.
Toronto

For Marion Seary

D.B.

For George L. MacDonald

K.M.D.

Kids Can Press Ltd. gratefully acknowledges the assistance of the Canada Council and the Ontario Arts Council in the production of this book.

Canadian Cataloguing in Publication Data

Main entry under title:

Til all the stars have fallen

ISBN 0-921103-90-5

1. Children's poetry, Canadian (English).*
I. Booth, David. II. Denton, Kady MacDonald

PS8273.T54 1989 jC811'.008'09282 C89-093105-4
PR9195.25.T54 1989

Kids Can Press Ltd.,
585½ Bloor Street West,
Toronto, Ontario, Canada, M6G 1K5.

Anthology title from the poem "This I Know". From *The Salamander's Laughter & Other Poems*, copyright © 1985 by Anne Corkett, published by Natural Heritage/Natural History Inc., Toronto, Canada

Book design by Michael Solomon
Typeset by Compeer Typographic Services Limited
Printed and bound in Hong Kong by Wing King Tong

89 0 9 8 7 6 5 4 3 2 1

Contents

Introduction

As a child, I loved to read poems. I even took out the entire poetry collection from the children's section of the Sarnia Public Library—one book at a time, of course.

How fortunate I am to be part of this book, for I have been able to reread many of the poems from my own childhood and to discover so many delightful new ones that belong to your generation. I read hundreds of poems in preparation, and each one that I selected spoke to me in some way. I have tried to arrange them by whatever quality first touched me in the poem—sometimes the pattern that set my toes tapping, sometimes the pictures that flooded my imagination, sometimes the spirit that filled my heart, sometimes the memories that filtered through my mind, and sometimes the story the poet told.

Kady MacDonald Denton, the artist who created the wonderful illustrations that accompany the poems, read each of the selections and then filled the page with her own responses to the poetry, and her pictures dance and fly right off the page.

Poets are wordsmiths, spending their lives choosing, bending, shaping, teasing, playing with words. The sounds of language fascinate them so. Poets write words that make your ears sing. When you read poems, they come alive with out-loud language. You can sometimes taste the words of a poem on your tongue as you make meaning in your imagination.

Poets shape their words into all kinds of patterns: grouping them into verses, fooling with punctuation, twisting the lines like pretzel ideas. Sometimes the poem's shape can help you hear what the poet is trying to say.

Poets take photographs of our country, our seasons, our weather, our people and ourselves without camera or film—pictures worth a thousand words. You may find yourself in the photo albums created by poets—black and white memories.

Read the poems in this collection and share the illustrations that surround them. Let them touch you like the first snowflakes of winter. Savour them, feel them, wonder about them, and find some more of them. Reread them if you want to. Say them aloud. Read one to a friend. Laugh if you feel like it. Forget some of them. Memorize some of them. Don't pick them apart (that hurts a poem). Copy down the ones you enjoy the most. Leave out the ones you don't understand or don't like. (Come back to them later; give them a second chance.) Write your own poems — those who read poems often want to write them. If a poet connects with you, read a whole book by that poet.

I didn't write these poems; I just borrowed them to help build this book for you. There were so many to choose from, hundreds of years of poems — enough for everyone.

David Booth

1989

WHEN YOUR EARS SING

This I know

The light of day
cannot stay.
The fading sun
will not come
to anybody's calling.

The cold moon light
Is clear and white.
She will not go,
this I know,
til all the stars have fallen.

Anne Corkett

Canadian Indian place names

Bella Bella, Bella Coola,
Athabaska, Iroquois;
Mesilinka, Osilinka,
Mississauga, Missisquois.
Chippewa, Chippawa,
Nottawasaga;
Malagash, Matchedash,
Shubenacadie;
Couchiching, Nipissing,
Scubenacadie.
Shickshock
Yahk
Quaw!

Meguido Zola

I get high on butterflies

I get high on butterflies;
the way they loom in the air
and land on air-dromes
                    of petals

and with nervous wings
shake off their colours
                    of orange, green and blue. . . .

I get high on butterflies;
their very names:
          Tiger swallow tail
          Zebra
          Pygmy blue
          Arctic skipper
          Spring azure
          Common wood nymph.

Caught in the net of my mind
they whirl around
          and around. . . .

Joe Rosenblatt

Nicholas tickle us

Nicholas Tickle us, make us all laugh,
"I will if you pay me a dime."
Too dear, Nicholas, cut that in half,
Just a nickel a tickle a time.

Sol Mandlsohn

The muddy puddle

I am sitting
In the middle
Of a rather Muddy
Puddle,
With my bottom
Full of bubbles
And my rubbers
Full of Mud,

While my jacket
And my sweater
Go on slowly
Getting wetter
As I very
Slowly settle
To the Bottom
Of the Mud.

And I find that
What a person
With a puddle
Round his middle
Thinks of mostly
In the muddle
Is the Muddi-
Ness of Mud.

Dennis Lee

Mischief City

A typical day in Mischief City,
The world's topsy-turvy, the world's out of whack.
They're looking at me and they're shaking their heads
And they say this all happened since I got back!

My name is Maxine, this is Mischief City,
Everything's damaged, soiled, busted or cracked.
My family is wishing they'd stayed in their beds
And I wish I could get my act back on its track!

My name is Maxine, *I'm* Mischief City,
I'm a runaway train that just ran out of track.
I'm a walking disaster, a giant whose tread
Leaves a trail of disaster, of ruin (and wrack)!

They're raising a statue in Mischief City,
It's a statue of me and my name's on the plaque.
I'm on top of this wrecking ball made out of lead
With a cloud overhead, and the cloud's painted black!

I've got to get out of Mischief City,
Before I reduce this old house to a shack.
I could move to the jungle, or maybe instead,
I'll just move in with you! Now how about that!

Tim Wynne-Jones

The sneeze

I winked and I blinked
And my nose got itchy
And my eyes all watered
And my mouth went twitchy
I went AHHHH
I went AHHHH
I went AHHHH **CHOOOOOO**
And I blew
And I sneezed
Then I coughed
And I wheezed
And my brother said, "Oh, brother!"
And my mother said,
"GAZOONTIGHT!"
My father said, "Bless you!"
And I said, Ah . . . ah . . . ah . . .
AHHHHHHHHHH **CHOOOOOOO!**

Sheree Fitch

The fox and the hounds

The fox
is happy he
is a fox

Except when
he is hounded
by hounds

The hounds
are happy they
are hounds

Especially when
they hound
the fox

When the fox
outfoxes
the hounds

He dreams
of being hounded
by more hounds

And the hounds
dream they are
those hounds

George Swede

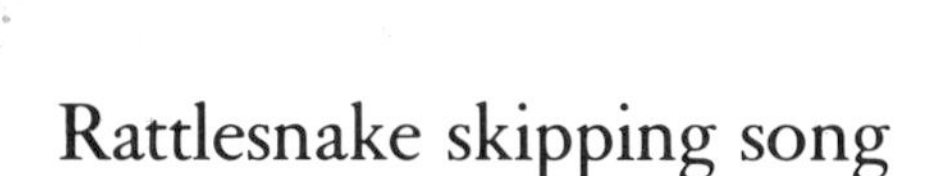

Rattlesnake skipping song

Mississauga rattlesnakes
Eat brown bread.
Mississauga rattlesnakes
Fall down dead.
If you catch a caterpillar
Feed him apple juice;
But if you catch a rattlesnake
Turn him loose!

Dennis Lee

Basso profundo

A singer, who sang
   in a deep basso key,
Lived three miles down
   in the Sargasso sea.
"I know it is hard to breathe,"
   said he,
"But no one in the world
   sings lower than me.
Glub diddy dum dum,
   glub diddy dee,
No one in the world
   sings lower than me!"

Sol Mandlsohn

Sea cliff

Wave on wave
and green on rock
and white between
the splash and black
the crash and hiss
of the feathery fall,
the snap and shock
of the water wall
and the wall of rock:
after—
after the ebb-flow,
wet rock,
high—
high over the slapping green,
water sliding away
and the rock abiding,
new rock riding
out of the spray.

A.J.M. Smith

Coyotes

The coyotes are howling;
it's forty below.
The moon is silvering
shivering snow.

Keeeipipipipiipipipipipipoo

kaiueoo oooo eeee yup

eeeeyayayayaya

oooooooooooooooooooooooooooooooooooooooooooooooooooooo

apapapapapapap

pukaaaaaa

keeoohahahahahahaahaahaa kyip

How many coyotes
do you think there are?
One for the moon
and one for each star.

aueeeeoooooooouiiiiuiwawawawawawawaiaiaiaiaiiaiiai

yute yieeyeet yite
eaeeeeeeeeeeeeeeeeeeeeeeeeeee

The coyotes are crying;
the night is awake
with their crying at midnight
on the frozen lake.

Jon Whyte

A path to the moon

From my front door there's a path to the moon
that nobody seems to see
tho it's marked with stones & grass & trees
there's nobody sees it but me.

You walk straight ahead for ten trees or so
turn left at the robin's song
follow the sound of the west wind down
past where the deer drink from the pond.

You take a right turn as the river bends
then where the clouds touch the earth
close your left eye & count up to ten
while twirling for all that you're worth.

And if you keep walking right straight ahead
clambering over the clouds
saying your mother's & father's names
over & over out loud

you'll come to the place where moonlight's born
the place where the moonbeams hide
and visit all of the crater sites
on the dark moon's secret side.

From my front door there's a path to the moon
that nobody seems to see
tho it's marked with stones & grass & trees
no one sees it but you & me.

bp Nichol

IN SILENT SNOW

December

round slice of moon: December night
stark branches lift
from hollowed black to silvered white
    no wind disturbs

the stars swing by in frozen flight
soft smoke floats thin
from fires alight in rooms below
    the stillness holds

in silent snow
neat footprints write a winter's tale
    the night dreams on

Fran Newman

November

sun
the
than
Snow higher
and fly
night geese
comes sky
down of
into ledge
the yellow
last

Anne Corkett

A tomato

t o m a t o
a t o m a t o m a t
a t o m a t o m a t o m a
a t o m a t o m a t o m a t
t o m a t o m a t o m a t o m a
t o m a t o m a t o m a t o m a
o m a t o m a t o m a t o m a t
m a t o m a t o m a t o m a t o m
a t o m a t o m a t o m a t o m a
o m a t o m a t o m a t o m a t
m a t o m a t o m a t o m a t o
a t o m a t o m a t o m a t o
o m a t o m a t o m a t o m
m a t o m a t o m a t o m
t o m a t o m a t o m
m a t o m a t o m
t o m a t o

Colin Morton

yawn

you know
i think
my favourite
thing in
the world
is
a
YAWN
i mean
everybody
does it
even
lizards
and
crocodiles
and i bet
if we only
knew
how
trees and
dandelions
do it too

as a matter
of fact
i bet
that when
all those
little
dandelion
fluffs blow
away
it's because
the dandelion
parent had
a great
big YAWN

and do you
know what
else is
great
YAWNS
are catching
i mean
when you
YAWN
then everybody
(or just about)
around you
YAWNS
and it
doesn't even
hurt
what a great
thing to give
to the world
a
YAWN

i bet
if all those
soldiers lined
up
facing each
other from
all the
countries
everywhere
in the world
and they were
all mad at
each other
i bet that
if just one
of them
YAWNED
the whole
world would be
safe

or
just imagine
if some bully
comes up
to you and
wants to
start a fight
just imagine
after all
the tough
stuff
all the
pushing
and making
faces
just imagine
if
just when he
was going to
pound you
you let out
a great big
YAWN

well
if that
didn't stop
him then
even if
he hit you
his fist
would go
right into
the middle
of your
YAWN
and if you
wanted to
you could bite
it off
of course
you wouldn't
have to
'cause everybody
would be
laughing so
hard
the fight would
be over

now
if you sneezed
at the same
time
imagine what
might
happen
●

sean o huigan

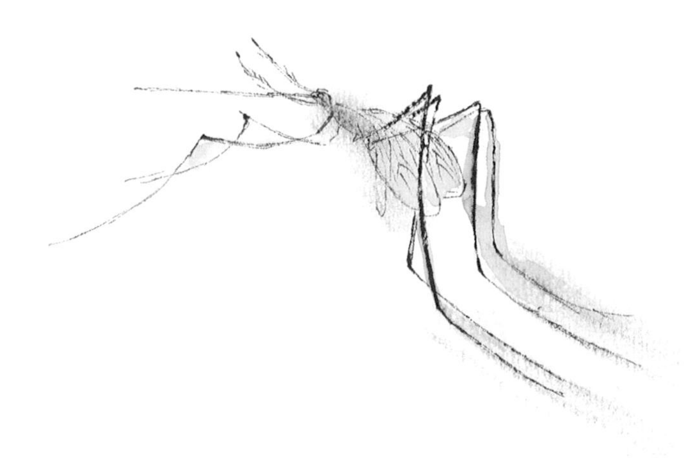

A mosquito in the cabin

Although you bash her,
swat her, smash her,
and go to bed victorious,
happy and glorious
she will come winging,
zooming and zinging,
wickedly singing
over your bed.
You slap the air
but she's in your hair
cackling with laughter.
You smack your head,
but she isn't dead—
she's on the rafter.
She's out for blood—
yours, my friend,
and she will get it, in the end.
She brings it first to boiling point,
then lets it steam.
With a fee, fi, fo and contented fum
she sips it
while you dream.

Myra Stilborn

Holes

Holes are shy and dull and round.
They're nothing, but don't remind them.
They live in sweaters, socks and crowns.
In flutes and Swiss cheese, holes abound.
And they hardly ever make a sound.
And some end up in the lost and found.
But most are buried in the ground,
You have to dig to find them.
Holes.

Tim Wynne-Jones

My toboggan and I carve winter

My toboggan and I carve winter
We crunch over the powdery snow
the one by one glistening grains
they sigh and squeak

then RACE
faster and faster
whipping the wind apart
carving jet trails with swirling tails
circling the shadow of every tree
nearing full flight
til
WHOMP!
a lurking bump tumbles us
into the drifts of freezing snow
We trudge slowly skyward for another run

Jane Wadley

Why/because

Why

did

i

j

u

m

p

from

the

school

s

tep

s

to

the

wb

o a

n n

s k?

Because

i

was

l

o

ne

l

y

Brian MacKinnon

The north wind

Once, when I was young I knew the wind.
I called "Wi-ind, North Wi-ind"
And it came,
  tramping the grass so that it lay flat,
And whinnied high and shrill like a whistle.
I saddled it with imagination,
  and bridled it with dreams.

And I got on and we went, and the trees
  bowed down in our passing.
I was exhilarated with the speed
  and lay down on his neck to keep
  balance.
And his snowy mane whipped about my face.
His unshod hoofs made no sound
  as he trod on the stars.
His breath made icicles on the houses
  we passed
And then he bucked.

Joanne Lysyk

HIGHER THAN THE SUN

Poems can give you

Poems can give you
double vision.
They make you see
the colours you feel
when you're sad,
the sound of a red,
red sunset,
the smells of happiness,
the flavours of the seasons,
Double vision
not blurred
but crisp as last night's snow.

Sandra Bogart

And my heart soars

The beauty of the trees,
the softness of the air,
the fragrance of the grass,
speaks to me.

The summit of the mountain,
the thunder of the sky,
the rhythm of the sea,
speaks to me.

The faintness of the stars,
the freshness of the morning,
the dew drop on the flower,
speaks to me.

The strength of fire,
the taste of salmon,
the trail of the sun,
And the life that never goes away,
They speak to me.

And my heart soars.

Chief Dan George

Think of the ocean . . .

think of the ocean
as a cat
with her grey fur
pushed
high upon her back
white boots
kneading the shore
on stormy days.

but
with the sun
shining
in a silk blue sky
she purrs
softly and her fur is
licked smooth and green
like the sand stone
she sleeps upon.

Siobhan Swayne

Fisherman

He is dark and wiry,
his bones, thin and sharp,
like the bones of the fish
in his net.
It seems as if
webbing grows on his fingers
and feet,
a starfish is his heart,
a seagull is his voice,
an oyster's pearl his eye,
he juts out of the sand
like a rock or some coral,
so long he has lived in the sea.

Dionne Brand

my friend

my friend is
like bark
rounding a tree

he warms
like sun
on a winter day

he cools
like water
in the hot noon

his voice
is ready
as a spring bird

he is
my friend
and I
am his

Emily Hearn

Hanging

High on the tree one apple alone
All her golden companions withered and gone.

Elizabeth Gourlay

Aesthetic curiosity

Does an owl appreciate
The color of leaves
As they fall about him
In the staggering nights of Autumn?

A.M. Klein

Jonathan's farm

I'd like a little farm
with a house that's painted blue,
with a lively little terrier
and a pussy cat or two.

I'd build a little barn
to keep my gentle cows,
outside I'd build a pig-pen
for piglets and for sows;

I'd plant a little orchard
with apple and with plum
and all the birds would praise
their green kingdom.

Miriam Waddington

October nights

October means it's Hallowe'en
When pumpkins don their faces,
And moans and groans and rattling bones
Are heard in haunted places.

When witches in their pointed hats
Go riding on their brooms,
And nighttime wears a velvet cloak
Of mystery and doom.

When graveyards start to come alive
With spirits of the dead,
It's such a lovely time of year
I think I'll stay in bed.

Harriet Cooper

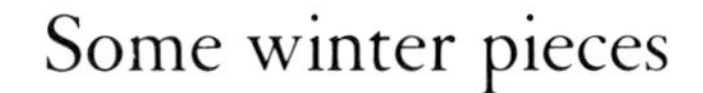

Some winter pieces

Tiny figures stand
Frozen, still, on clean white snow.
Green ice pond, black trees.

So cold this morning,
Snow squeaks, crunches underfoot;
Steam ghosts dance on drains.

In my back garden:
Footprints of rabbits,
And a frozen dead starling.

Ice-coated maple
Groans slightly in wintersleep;
Yawns out one green shoot.

In late afternoon
Snow glows pink, pale sky burns cold;
Black shadows lengthen.

William H. Moore

Winter yard

Bundled,
eyes watering against the glare,
we wade
into the crusty winter yard.
Bushes hang heavy
with suet-soaked onion bags.
Pine cones drip peanutbutter and seeds.
Coconuts hang by their eyes
and Javex bottles swing crazy
on the clothesline.
We smile
red tight
and closed with cold
and retreat to wait.

Shoulder to shoulder with cat at the window,
noses pressed on fogged-up glass,
we watch,
impatient.
Erin calls,
"Birds! Come here! We have seeds for you!"
Gulls sweep the sky.
Starlings crowd the neighbouring maples.
Jays scream.
Hundreds of wings beat the air,
and
then
they
descend.

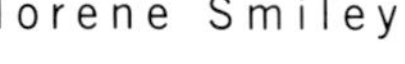

Norene Smiley

Laughter

We are light
as dandelion
parachutes we
land anywhere
take the shape
of wherever we
fall

we are often
the size of
grasshoppers in
a jungle of grass
or we're squirmy
chains of willow
catkins

then we become
curly seashells
knobby little
swimmers in a
sea of air
lying

on our backs
our eyes fly up
higher than kites
airplanes clouds
winds higher
than stars and

we stare down
at the little
distant world
and we laugh
laugh laugh

Miriam Waddington

Field in the wind

The grass is running in the wind
Without a sound,
Crouching and smooth and fast
Along the ground.
The clouds run too,
And little shadows play
And scurry in the grass
That will not stay
But runs and runs, until
The wind is still.

Floris Clark McLaren

The yellow tulip

For weeks
it struggled
through the hard crust
of the spring earth
and a foot
of air

Just to be
scorched
by the sun
jolted
by raindrops
blasted
by the wind

But on this gentle
May morning
as it opens
yellow petals
to the sky

Nothing else matters

George Swede

Silverly

Silverly,
  Silverly,
Over the
  Trees
The moon drifts
  By on a
Runaway
  Breeze.

Dozily,
  Dozily,
Deep in her
  Bed,
A little girl
  Dreams with the
Moon in her
  Head.

Dennis Lee

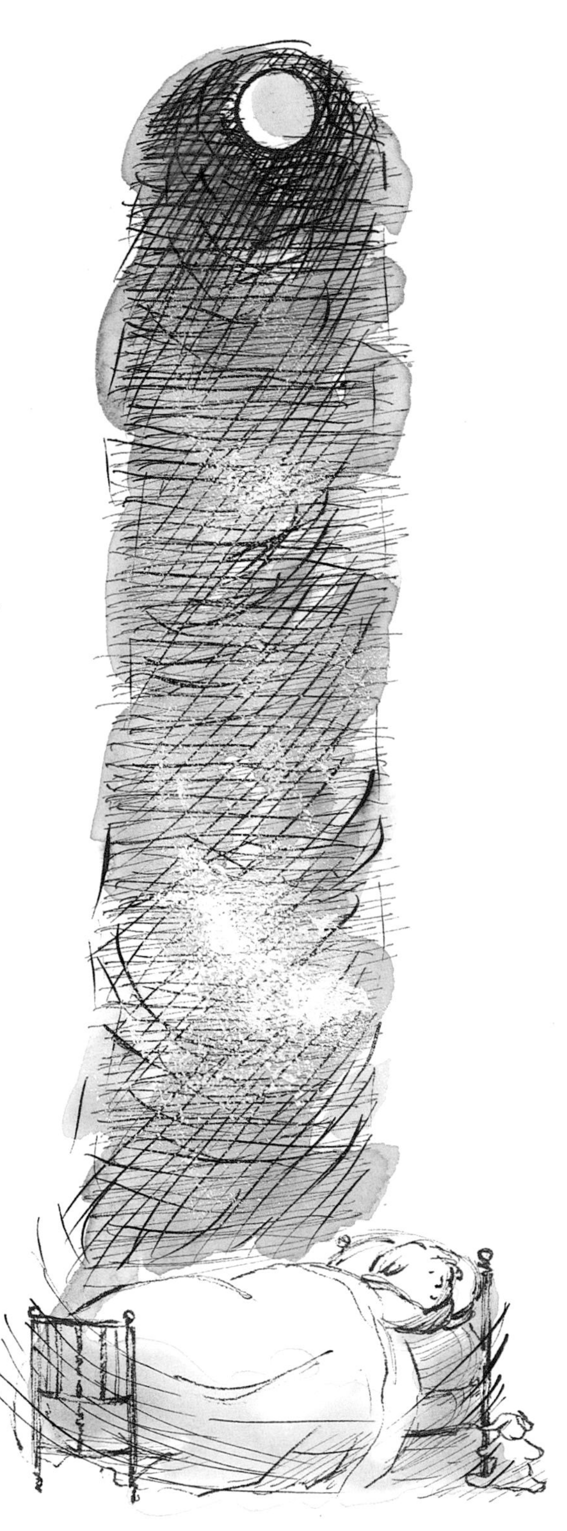

EVERYTHING IN ITS PLACE

Squirrels in my notebook

I went to Stanley Park
to put squirrels in my notebook
My teacher said
write everything you found out
about squirrels

and so I will

I saw a fat one
shaped like a peanut butter jar
attacking my hat

his moustache was made of chips
he ran sideways into the sky

He looked like a ginger cat
with a branch for a tail

He was so mad he ran down again
and I can't write
what he said to me

Lucky for me I had a sandwich
to share with him

He smiled at me till his teeth
weren't hungry
and jumped into the sky
with his jammy legs

he turned into
a kite.

Florence McNeil

Every morning

Every morning
I awake
full of dust
and odors

As if
no one has
lived in me
for years

And
every morning
I throw open
all my windows
and doors

Clean
and fumigate
myself

As if
I were just
moving in

George Swede

Courage

Courage is when you're
allergic to cats and

your new friend says can
you come to her house to
play after school and

stay to dinner then
maybe go skating and
sleep overnight? And,

she adds, you can pet
her small kittens! Oh,
how you ache to. It

takes courage to
say "no" to all that.

Emily Hearn

Tinkering

I love beginning with
a clean sheet and
laying down each grease-black
cog and bolt and link
aligning positions
adjusting tensions and
checking for wear.

I love finishing in
reverse order and
picking up each clean, oiled
sprocket, nut and washer
spinning the wheel
and hearing only the whirr
of everything in place.

Diane Dawber

Names don't always suit

Two cats live in the house
Across the street from us,
One cat is black,
The other is white.

At night I hear their owner
Calling them home.
"Coalbin," she calls the dark one.
"Winter," she calls the white.

But names don't always suit,
for Coalbin shines like silk
From washing herself,
And how can we call
Winter in summer?

Nancy Prasad

Jeremy's house

Jeremy hasn't a roof on his house
For he likes to look at the stars;
When he lies in his bed
With them all overhead
He imagines that he can see Mars.

Sometimes a thunderstorm lights up the sky
And Jeremy gets soaking wet;
But he says that it's worth it
To lie in his bed
And see folks go past in a jet.

He's counting the stars in the Milky Way,
It's going to take him forever;
But Jeremy's patiently
Counting away
For he knows it's a worthwhile endeavour.

Lois Simmie

Thrum drew a small map

Thrum drew
A small map

He put in
The small countries
The lizards and
The bugs and
The snails and
The worms

He made a mountain
And a green tree
And small rocks
And smaller rocks

He made a river
And a little fish

He made a meadow
And a little mouse

He made specks
That were ants
He made a queer smile
On the countenance of
A bee

He made a person
Small as a
Minnow

He made white birds
In a blue sky
But because he had no
Yellow
He couldn't draw the sun

He made an ocean
And a small boat

He made daytime and
Nighttime and a
Small evening star

He signed his name
In small letters
At the bottom
Almost too small
To be able to
See

He loved his small
Map
With its small
Small secrets

Grim came and tore it
Up

Susan Musgrave

Waiting for the first drop

No-one knows the exact moment
of what hour
the first drop of rain will fall.

But after one whole week
of blinding sun
of scorched grass
of wilting leaves,
it somehow seems important.

So I watch and wait
along with the birds,
along with the ants,
along with every living
breathing thing,

for that first heavy
cool splash of rain
to wet the page
of this poem about the rain.

Raymond Souster

Winter walk in forest

All else
is so
perfectly still
my breathing sounds
like gusts of wind
my joints
like frozen branches
cracking

All around me
invisible animals
must also be listening

But only
to how close
my boots
snap the snowcrust

George Swede

Recipe for Thanksgiving Day soup

today i made soup
on the woodstove—
with a snap of frost in the air,
a fire feels good—
  i started it off
with a soup bone
from the general store—
can't sell soup bones up here,
they give them away—this one
had great chunks of gristle
and beef on it
  —beautiful—
set it to simmer
at the back of the stove
in fresh water, threw in
onion and thyme from the garden,
a few celery leaves
bits of green pepper,
bay leaf, salt—
  it's the spring water brings out
  the goodness

meantime i filled up
the woodbox with stovelengths
i buzzed split and piled
from logs the neighbour's kid
  helped me haul up
from the gully
the woodshed is bulging
to get back to the soup—
while the stock was cooking
i diced up the rest of the vegetables:
  potatoes, tomatoes, carrots,
  a little more onion,
  peas, beans—
all grown thru the summer
and stored in the cellar—
  threw in a handful
  of wild rice
  for body
took out the soup bone, cut up
the meat and put it back in
saved the bone for
the neighbour's kids' dog

simmered the broth
to a rich autumn brown
  stirring occasionally
  with a big wooden spoon
  and tasting for flavour

called in the neighbours
to share it
we ate it with fresh
homemade bread
they brought over
  sure was good soup

Dorothy Farmiloe

The sky is falling

It's cool under the August
apple tree
and fun
lying on my back looking
at the sky
    shaped into blue chunks
      between leaves
    magnified
      between fingers
    rainbowed
      between eyelashes.
You can see a lot
everything but the apple
that hits your nose
and then nothing but
       stars.

Diane Dawber

Nature

As the orange-
striped cat
hunches,
glaring down,

the pale-fluffed
nestlings
he's discovered
feel cooled
in the shadow,

and

stretch their thin
necks, heavy
heads up,
hungry
beaks open,

wide
on hinges.

Milton Acorn

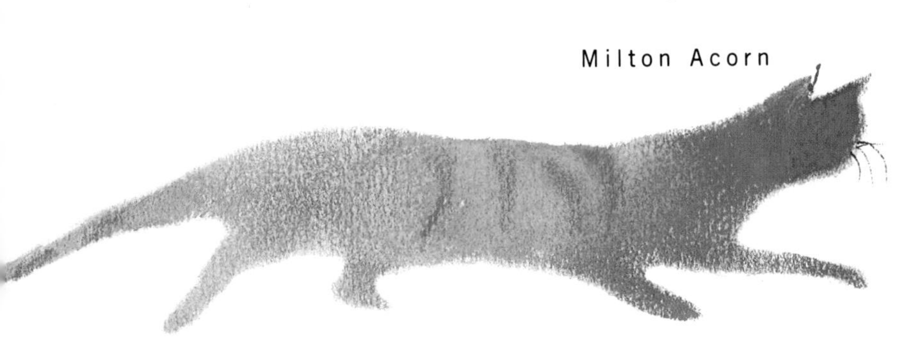

ALL MY SECRETS

If you don't come

The sun will get
smaller and smaller
and the grass won't green
or the trees leaf
and there will be
no flowers or birdsong.

The winds will blow cold
and the nights will be dark
without moonlight or stars

for there will be
no summer here
if you don't come.

Marguerite Mack

Fingerprint

My grandparents' kitchen
smelled of soap
      always soap
      and carrots

My grandmother performed
rituals in the kitchen
She had a man's hands
      but smooth
as if her fingerprints
had been worn down
levelled like old hills

My hands in her hands
working the soap
with a strong grip

Harry Thurston

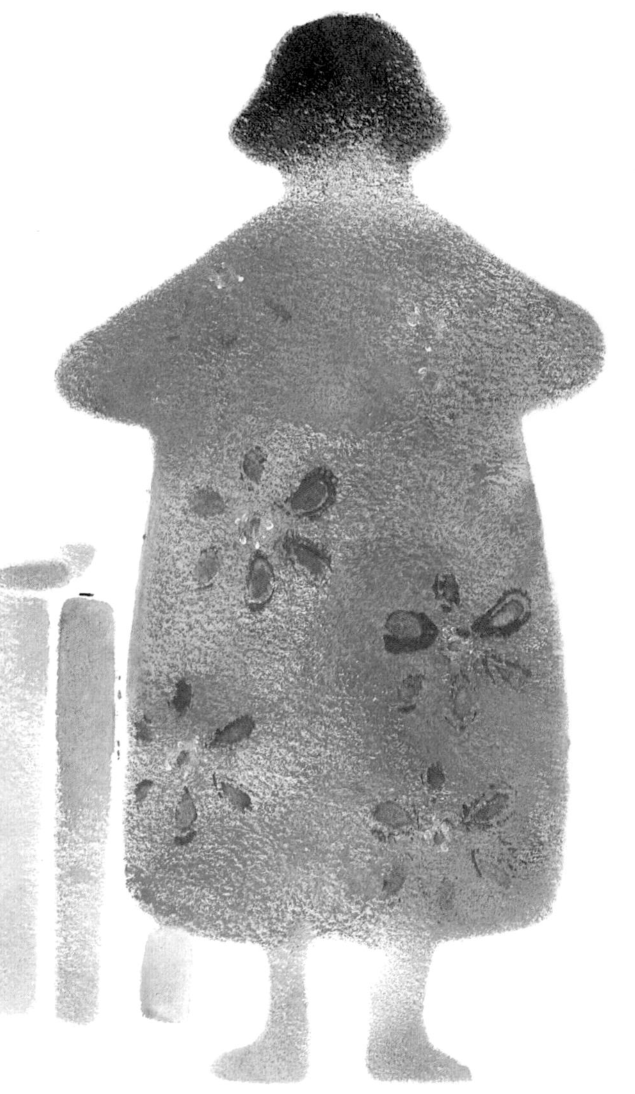

Long, long ago

It seems I always saw the Indian woman
the instant she became visible,
and never took my eyes off her
as she lugged her many-coloured pack,
three times as big as herself,
down South Mountain,
across Little Bridge,
up North Mountain
and into our kitchen
where she undid a knot
and flooded the entire room with baskets
—cherry-coloured baskets,
wheat-coloured baskets,
cabbage-coloured baskets,
baskets the colour of a November sky,
each basket containing
another, smaller basket,
down to one so tiny it would hold
only a hang of thread and a thimble.

Alden Nowlan

Snake woman

I was once the snake woman,

the only person, it seems, in the whole place
who wasn't terrified of them.

I used to hunt with two sticks
among milkweed and under porches and logs
for this vein of cool green metal
which would run through my fingers like mercury
or turn to a raw bracelet
gripping my wrist:

I could follow them by their odour,
a sick smell, acid and glandular,
part skunk, part inside
of a torn stomach,
the smell of their fear.

Once caught, I'd carry them,
limp and terrorized, into the dining room,
something even men were afraid of.
What fun I had!
Put that thing in my bed and I'll kill you.

Now, I don't know.
Now I'd consider the snake.

Margaret Atwood

The roundhouse

That first real year
I pitched baseball
we played straight across
from the roundhouse on St. Clair,

and every time
I got jammed up good
in a three-and-two count,
I'd simply stall a little
till a black screen of smoke
blew across from its chimney,
then wind up and throw one
right down the gut
with no worries at all. . . .

But like everything else
that was too good to last—
the next year they tore down
my handy old roundhouse,
and I only finished seven
of my fifteen starts,

all the smoke gone forever
you might say
from my fast one.

Raymond Souster

Together

Lying in bed
next to my mother.
This has to be the best,
the very best thing.
We are reading.
Dad is away
"Want an apple?"
and she bites in.
Crack, crack,
go her jaws
like a hinged fence
that doesn't work right.
I try not to listen
to those hinged jaws
I can't read
I've never noticed
my mother's jaws
doing that before
"Maybe it's the way
she's lying," I think to myself.
"Gee, you eat
apples funny,"
I finally blurt out.

She doesn't say anything.
She just looks at me
awful quiet
and puts the apple
on the bed stead
behind her.

We continue to read
in silence.

That was two years ago.

But it feels like
last night
the two of us
reading in bed

My mother
no longer eating
and I,
wishing, oh, wishing
wishing she were.

Carolyn Mamchur

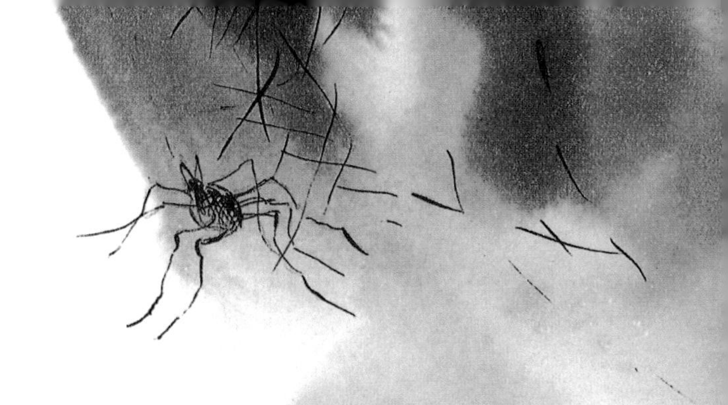

The visitor

one night
i woke up
when the
rest were
asleep
and felt
something
crawly
that started
to creep
up my arm
'neath the
covers
i brushed
it away
but it
didn't go
it wanted
to stay
it creepy
crawled
slowly
with long
hairy
steps
it tickled
and
whispered
and got to
my neck
it sssssssed
and it husssshhhhhed
and it ssssshhhhhhhhhed
and it haaaaaaaahhhhed
it creeped 'cross
my face
and it felt
very odd
it crawled
'round my shoulders
and crept down
my back
then spidered
away
and hid
in the
black

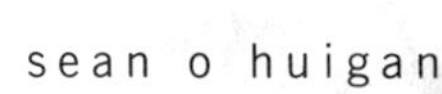

sean o huigan

And even now

When I was a child,
Lying in bed on a summer evening,
The wind was a tall sweet woman
Standing beside my window.
She came whenever my mind was quiet.

But on other nights
I was tossed about in fear and agony
Because of goblins poking at the blind,
And fearful faces underneath my bed.
We played a horrible game of hide-and-seek
With Sleep the far-off, treacherous goal.

And even now, stumbling about in the dark,
I wonder, Who was it that touched me?—
What thing laughed?

Dorothy Livesay

The royal visit

When the King and the Queen came to Stratford
Everyone felt at once
How heavy the Crown must be.
The Mayor shook hands with their Majesties
And everyone presentable was presented
And those who weren't have resented
It, and will
To their dying day.
Everyone had almost a religious experience
When the King and Queen came to visit us
(I wonder what they felt!)
And hydrants flowed water in the gutters
All day.
People put quarters on the railroad tracks
So as to get squashed by the Royal Train
And some people up the line at Shakespeare
Stayed in Shakespeare, just in case—
They did stop too,
While thousands in Stratford
Didn't even see them
Because the Engineer didn't slow down
Enough in time.
And although,
But although we didn't see them in any way
(I didn't even catch the glimpse
The teacher who was taller did
Of a gracious pink figure)
I'll remember it to my dying day.

James Reaney

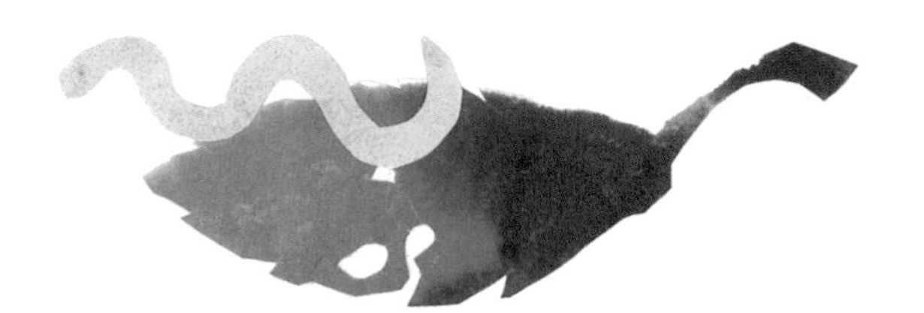

Smart remark

When my older sister Marilyn
came for a visit,
She spent most of her time trying
to make us over
Into some other kind of family.
The kind you see on TV who get all
excited and beam
Because they're having Lipton's
Chicken Noodle soup for
supper.
The kind who pick to spend the
whole day in the new Mall.
The kind who love to do things
together and talk non-stop.
The kind we aren't.
When she said, for the fifteenth
time,
"Kate, must you always have your
head in a book?"
The worm turned and I snapped,
"Yes. I must.
It's better than having no head
—Like you!"

Dad laughed.
Mother sent me to my room.

Afterwards, she said,
"It was clever, Kate. It may even
have been true.
But you didn't have to hurt her."

"She hurt ME!" I complained.
"Did she really?" Mother asked,
looking me in the eye.
"Oh, I guess not," I said, thinking
back over the visit.
"But she drove me crazy, picking at
me . . . and . . ."

"You wanted to swat her," Mother
finished for me.
"So did we all. But you don't swat
butterflies, Kate."
"If she's a butterfly, what am I?" I
demanded.
"A mosquito," my father joined in.
"But Marilyn's not exactly a
butterfly, April.
She's more like a . . . tent
caterpillar."

Mother laughed.
Why didn't she send HIM to his
room?

I know why.
He said it when Marilyn couldn't
hear.
In other words, behind her back.
Which makes him a spider?

And Mother . . . a . . . a . . .
Queen Bee, I suppose.

Jean Little

VOICES ON THE WIND

Orders

Muffle the wind;
Silence the clock;
Muzzle the mice;
Curb the small talk;
Cure the hinge-squeak;
Banish the thunder.
Let me sit silent,
Let me wonder.

A.M. Klein

Hurricane

Shut the windows
Bolt the doors
Big rain coming
Climbing up the mountain.

Neighbours whisper
Dark clouds gather
Big rain coming
Climbing up the mountain.

Gather in the clothes lines
Pull down the blinds
Big wind rising
Coming up the mountain.

Branches falling
Raindrops flying
Tree tops swaying
People running
Big wind blowing
Hurricane! on the mountain.

Dionne Brand

Windlady

Nine miles high
You drag me, your raindoll by
Till I've cried the rivers full
Windlady, weatherwinder, windsteeple
Windhat, windoldpaper, windowsill
Across the mountain, across the sea
        Wind me

James Reaney

My moccasins have not walked

My moccasins have not walked
Among the giant forest trees

My leggings have not brushed
Against the fern and berry bush

My medicine pouch has not been filled
with roots and herbs and sweetgrass

My hands have not fondled the spotted fawn

My eyes have not beheld
The golden rainbow of the north

My hair has not been adorned
With the eagle feather

Yet
My dreams are dreams of these
My heart is one with them
The scent of them caresses my soul

Duke Redbird

Zeroing in

The tree down the street
 has little green apples
  that never get bigger
   never turn red.
They just drop on the ground
 get worm holes
  brown spots.
They're
 just right for stepping on
  like walking on bumpy marbles,
   or green eggs that break with a snap
    just right for gathering
     in a heap behind the hedge
      waiting
       for a target.
Here comes my brother.

Diane Dawber

Here comes the witch

Here comes the witch.
    Don't make a sound.
Here comes the witch.
    Don't turn around.
Stand as still as still can be.
Like a statue, like a tree.
She's bony, warty, green-faced too,
Hungry for someone just like you.

Here comes the witch.
    She's very near.
Here comes the witch.
    She's now right here.
She's reaching out! She caught your eye!
Now raise your arms and *fly*, *fly*, *fly*!

Robert Heidbreder

You better be ready

What are all those rocks sticking up for? he says.
Those are markers for graves.
Graves?
Where they bury people, after you die.
No, you are wrong, Uncle Johnny. When you die, God
  takes you away in a car.
Whereabouts?
Whereabouts?
Yes. Whereabouts does God take you?
It's a secret, he says.
Well, there are people buried right there!
I know, Uncle Johnny. But they just missed their ride,
  that's all.
Oh, I say.

John Lane

Licorice

For those who want the recipe
I give it to you here for free:
First you take a running shoe
And boil it for a day or two,
And when it's turned a greyish goo
You add the ink (in navy blue).
Erasers (lots), hairnets (a few),
Three rubber boots (two old, one new);
Then let the mixture steam and stew
At least one week (no more than two);
Then take a sieve and strain it through
And let it cool; in three days chew
And if it doesn't quite agree
Send me back the recipe.

John Paul Duggan

Unicorn

Unicorn, Unicorn,
where have you gone?
I've brought you some silver dew
out of the dawn.
I've put it in buttercups
for you to drink
and brought you some daisies
to wear round your neck.

Silver and gold
and petals so white,
these are the colours
saved from the night.

Unicorn, Unicorn,
where have you gone?
I've brought you nine sunbeams
to wear for a crown
and made you a blanket
of new thistledown
embroidered with lilies—
O where have you gone?
Unicorn, Unicorn,
I can't stay long.

Petals so white
and silver and gold,
these are the colours
that never grow old.

Anne Corkett

July

Lie on your front in the summer sand;
Bake for as long as you can stand.

Lie on your back, let the heat soak in;
Then roll around on your summer skin.

Lie on your side to enjoy the view;
Ease yourself over to toast side two.

Run to escape the blazing sun . . .
It's too late—you're overdone!

Fran Newman

Anxious

Anxious
of course I'm anxious
afraid
of course I'm afraid
I don't know what about
I don't know what of
but I'm afraid
and I feel it's
right to be.

Miriam Waddington

WHISTLING IN THE DARK

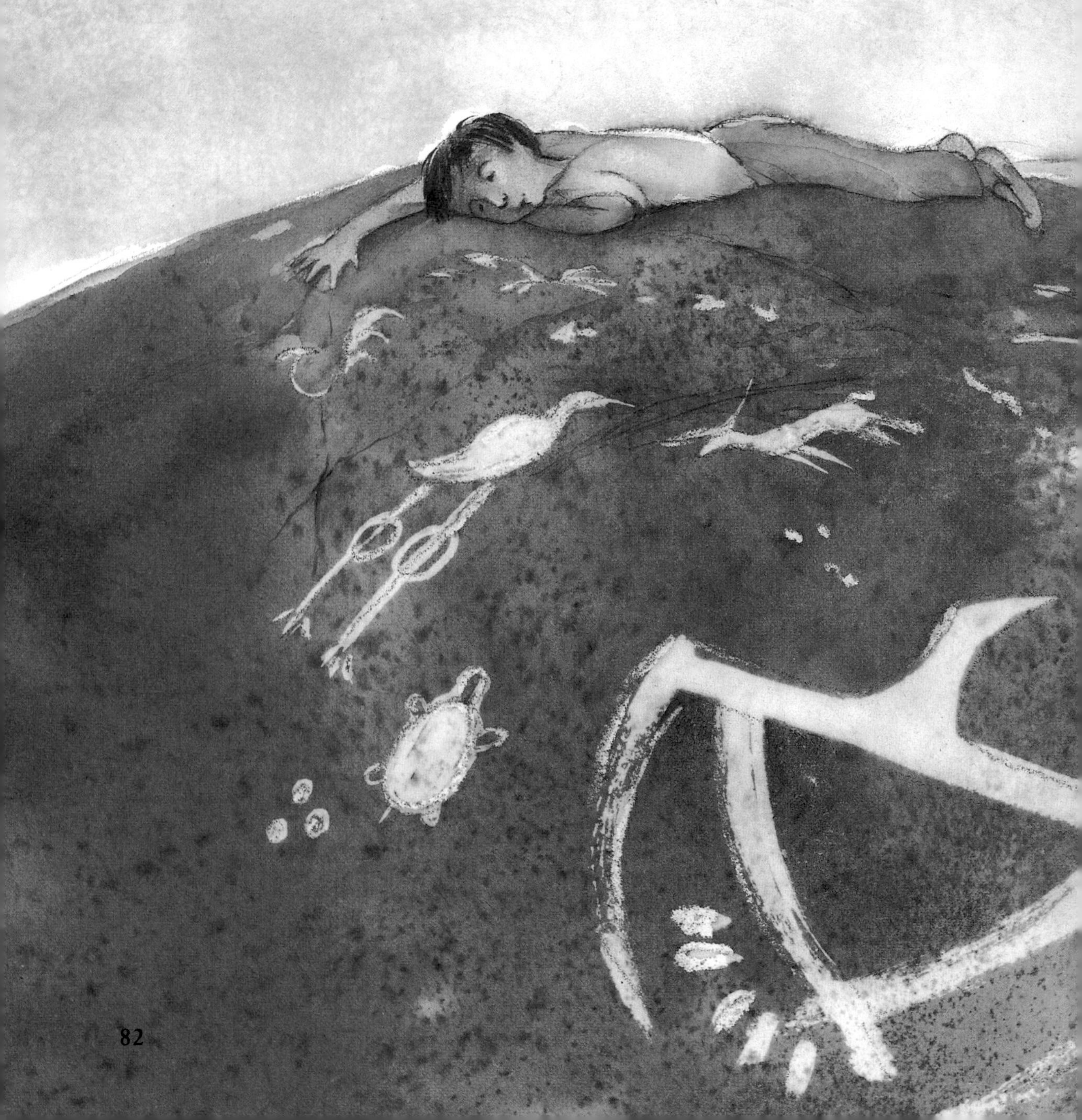

Drums of my father

A hundred thousand years have passed
Yet, I hear the distant beat of my father's drums.
I hear his drums throughout the land,
His beat I feel within my heart.

The drums shall beat, so my heart shall beat,
And I shall live a hundred thousand years.

Shirley Daniels

Too hot to sleep

He was sleeping when bear
came down from the mountain
by the water trap
after cleaning the screen
of branches and gravel

He fell asleep, a hot june morning
above Wapta Lake, the Kicking Horse Pass
When Muskwa came down without a sound
And snuffed at his jeans

Who's this asleep on my mountain?

It's my friend Birnie asleep I said
(in my head)
I didn't hear you coming bear
I was dozing, I looked up
and there you were

You never know said Bear
just where the wind will lead me
when I'll be around
or what beat I'm hunting on

and sniffed at Birnie's collar
at his ear, which he licked tentatively
causing Birnie to moan softly

Nothing doing here he said, nothing doing

"We were just going bear," I said quietly
edging backwards

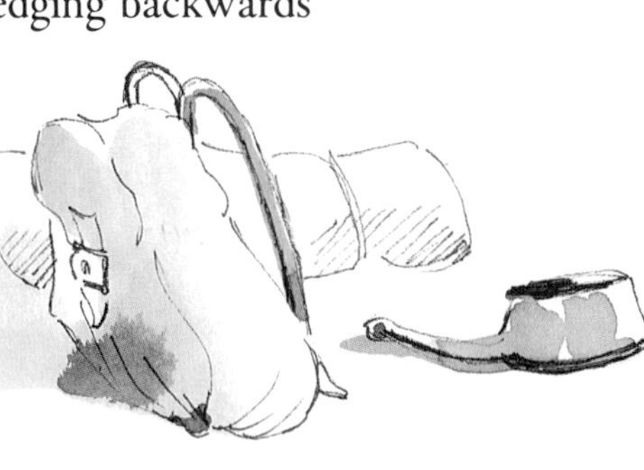

Don't move too quickly will you, said Bear
when you move, or better still
don't move at all

Are you here often, are you coming again?
he asked, flipping over a stone
licking delicately the underside
"No," I said. good he said, that's good.

I just came down from the pass
the wind blowing up my nose
to see who was sleeping on my mountain
he said, and sniffed at Birnie's armpit
Whoosh   whoosh he snorted

and turned away, clattered down the creek
popping his teeth, his hackles up
Went out of sight
around the shoulder of Mount Hector

as Birnie woke rubbing his eyes
"Too hot to sleep he said." Yeah.

Sid Marty

The dinosaur dinner

Allosaurus, stegosaurus,
Brontosaurus too,
All went off for dinner at the
Dinosaur zoo;

Along came the waiter called
Tyrannosaurus Rex,
Gobbled up the table
'Cause they wouldn't pay their checks.

Dennis Lee

Trip to the seashore

We drove to the seashore,
My ma and pa,
Brother Bertie
And Sue and me;
From Biggar, Saskatchewan,
Over the mountains,
What did we see?
We saw the sea.

Sister Sue said
"Isn't it big?
It's bigger than Biggar
Or anything yet."
Brother Bertie
Up to his knees,
And Ma to her ankles
Said "Isn't it wet?"

I let out a yelp
When I saw kelp
And a scuttling crab,
Pa laughed at that;
He sat on the land
With his toes in the sand,
"I'll be darned," he said,
"Isn't it flat?"

At the seafood restaurant
Ma had oysters,
They looked horrid,
Green and squishy;

There were boats through the window,
Sue had scallops,
(Pa said we had to have
Something fishy).

Bertie had lobster,
I had crab,
We looked through the window
At waves and foam;
Pa had whisky
And fish and chips,
He said, "We've seen it,
Let's go home."

We drove all day
We travelled all night,
The parents and Sue
And Bertie and I;
We fought over comics
And seashells and Pa yelled
"Look at the mountains!
Aren't they high?"

We got home to Biggar,
Ma and Pa,
Sister Sue
And Bertie and me;
Pa said "Look,
Isn't it beautiful?
Big and flat,
Just like the sea."

Lois Simmie

Windigo spirit

The Windigo is a spirit of the North, the Cree told us.
The Windigo is a cannibal spirit, the Cree told us.
The Windigo will possess a man
  form ice inside his soul
  cause fur to cover his skin
  create a craving for human flesh
The Cree told us,
Two bitter nights ago.
Two nights ago, we left their dismal camp, to check
Our traplines. It was twenty-below-zero
Two nights ago, but now it has gotten
Really cold. Windigo, Windigo,
Passing through our thoughts
Like wind at thirty-five below.
Windigo.
The Windigo moves thru the five moons of winter
  shrouded in a blizzard
  blown by high winds over frozen lakes
  or creeps inexorably on
  thru those still days
  when life is locked immutable in minus
  fifty skies, those cloudless, breathless
  days when neither air nor man dare move.
The Windigo crosses a portage
  then a sun-blind lake
  then the soul of any fool
  alone
    out here,
      like us

Now.
Two nights out, out from another man, we are still
Strangers in front of our fire,
our meek fire melting
melting just enough
night air
to breathe.
A shadow moves.
Windigo.
Two nights ago, the Cree told of a trapper lost,
Near here,
Now surely, host of
The Windigo Spirit.
Cold.
Windigo. Windigo.
Two nights out, the dead trapper enters the ring of our fire
his own lips and fingers chewed off in hunger
a gaping chasm of a mouth ringed with frozen
Blood.
Two nights out, I turn to my companion,
behind his eyes ice forms
his hands are matted with hair
This night, I rise and scream.
My scream crosses the frozen lake and dies somewhere in the spruce
dies somewhere in the spruce.
Windigo. Windigo.
Windigo.

Ken Stange

Paul Bunyan

He came,
striding
over the mountain,
the moon slung on his back,
like a pack,
a great pine
stuck on his shoulder
swayed as he
talked
to his blue ox
Babe;
a huge, looming shadow
of a man,
clad
in a mackinaw coat,
his logger's shirt
open at the throat
and the great mane of hair
matching, meeting
the locks of night,
the smoke from his cauldron pipe,
a cloud on the moon
and his laugh
rolled through the mountains
like thunder
on a summer night
while the lightning of his smile
split the heavens
asunder.
His blue ox, Babe,
pawed the ground
till the earth
trembled
and shook
and a high cliff
toppled and fell;
and Babe's bellow
was fellow
to the echo
of Bunyan's laughter;
and then
with one step
he was in the next valley
dragging the moon after,
the stars
tangled,
spangled
in the branches of the great pine.
And as he left,
he whistled in the dark
like a far off train
blowing for a crossing
and plainly heard
were the plodding grunts
of Babe, the blue ox,
trying
to keep pace
from hill to hill,
and then, the sounds,
fading,
dying,
were lost
in the churn of night,—
and all was still.

Arthur S. Bourinot

Acknowledgements

Grateful acknowledgement is made to the publishers, authors and other copyright holders who have granted permission to reprint copyrighted material.

Every reasonable effort has been made to locate the copyright holders for these poems. The publishers would be pleased to receive information that would allow them to rectify any omissions in future printings.

- "This I know", "November" and "Unicorn": From *The Salamander's Laughter & Other Poems* by Anne Corkett, copyright © 1985. Reprinted by permission of Natural Heritage/Natural History Inc., Toronto, Canada.
- "Canadian Indian place names": By Meguido Zola. From *Here Is a Poem*, published by the League of Canadian Poets, copyright © 1983. Reprinted by permission of the author.
- "I get high on butterflies": From *Top Soil* by Joe Rosenblatt, copyright © 1976. Reprinted by permission of Press Porcépic Limited and the author.
- "Nicholas tickle us" and "Basso Profundo": From *Nicholas Tickle Us*, published by PMA Publishers, Toronto, Canada, copyright © 1985 by Sol Mandlsohn. Reprinted by permission of the author.
- "The muddy puddle": From *Garbage Delight* by Dennis Lee, copyright © 1977. Reprinted by permission of Macmillan of Canada, A Division of Canada Publishing Corporation.
- "Mischief City" and "Holes": From *Mischief City*, copyright © Tim Wynne-Jones 1986. A Groundwood Book, Douglas & McIntyre. Reprinted by permission of the publisher.
- "The sneeze": From *Toes in My Nose*, copyright © 1987 by Sheree Fitch. Reprinted by permission of Doubleday Canada Ltd.
- "The fox and the hounds": By George Swede. From *High Wire Spider*, Three Trees Press, copyright © 1986. Reprinted by permission of the author.
- "Rattlesnake skipping song": From *Alligator Pie* by Dennis Lee, copyright © 1974. Reprinted by permission of Macmillan of Canada, A Division of Canada Publishing Corporation.
- "Sea cliff:" From *The Classic Shade* by A.J.M. Smith, copyright © 1978. Reprinted by permission of the Canadian Publishers, McClelland and Stewart, Toronto.
- "Coyotes": By Jon Whyte. From *Prairie Jungle*, edited by Wenda McArthur and Geoffrey Ursel, copyright © 1985. Reprinted by permission of Coteau Books, Regina, Canada.
- "A path to the moon": From *Giant Moonquakes and Other Disasters*, copyright © 1985 by bp Nichol. Reprinted by permission of Black Moss Press.
- "December" and "July": From *Sunflakes and Snowshine*, copyright © 1977 by Fran Newman and Claudette Boulanger. Reprinted by permission of Scholastic-TAB Publications Ltd.
- "A tomato": By Colin Morton. From *Here Is a Poem*, published by the League of Canadian Poets, copyright © 1983. Reprinted by permission of the author.
- "Yawn:" From *Well You Can Imagine* by sean o huigan, copyright © 1983. Reprinted by permission of Black Moss Press.
- "A mosquito in the cabin": By Myra Stilborn. From *Round Slice of Moon*, copyright © 1980, Scholastic-TAB.
- "My toboggan and I carve winter": By Jane Wadley. From *Round Slice of Moon*, copyright © 1980, Scholastic-TAB.
- "Why/Because": By Brian MacKinnon. From *Here Is a Poem*, published by the League of Canadian Poets, copyright © 1983.
- "The north wind": By Joanne Lysyk. From *Pandora's Box*, published by The Canadian Council of Teachers of English.
- "Poems can give you": By Sandra Bogart. From *Round Slice of Moon*, copyright © 1980 by Scholastic-TAB Publications Ltd. Reprinted by permission of the publisher.
- "And my heart soars": By Chief Dan George. Copyright © 1974 by Chief Dan George and Helmut Hirnschall. Reprinted by permission of Hancock House Publishing Ltd. 19313 Zero Avenue, Surrey, B.C. V3S 5J9
- "Think of the ocean": By Siobhan Swayne. From *Here Is a Poem*, published by the League of Canadian Poets, copyright © 1983. Reprinted by permission of the author.
- "Fisherman" and "Hurricane": From *Earth Magic*, copyright © 1979 by Dionne Brand. Reprinted by permission of the author.
- "My friend" and "Courage": By Emily Hearn from *Hockey Cards and Hopscotch*, copyright © 1980 by Nelson Canada. Reprinted by permission of Nelson Canada.
- "Hanging": From *To Say the Least*, copyright © 1979 by Elizabeth Gourlay, Press Porcépic Ltd. Reprinted by permission of the author.
- "Aesthetic curiosity" and "Orders": From *The Collected Poems of A.M. Klein*, copyright © 1974. Reprinted by permission of McGraw-Hill Ryerson Limited.
- "Jonathan's farm": This poem appears in *Collected Poems*, copyright © 1986 by Miriam Waddington, with the title "Child's Poem". Reprinted by permission of Oxford University Press.
- "October nights": By Harriet Cooper. From *Here Is a Poem*, published by the League of Canadian Poets, copyright © 1983.
- "Some winter pieces": By William H. Moore. Published by permission of the author.
- "Winter yard": By Norene Smiley. From *Seaweed in Your Stocking*, copyright © 1985. Reprinted by permission of the Children's Writers' Workshop.
- "Laughter" and "Anxious": From *Collected Poems*, copyright © 1986 by Miriam Waddington. Reprinted by permission of Oxford University Press Canada.
- "Field in the wind": From *Frozen Fire*, copyright © 1937 by Floris Clark McLaren.
- "The yellow tulip", "Every morning" and "Winter walk in forest": By George Swede. From *Time Flies*, Three Trees Press, copyright © 1984. Reprinted by permission of the author.
- "Silverly" and "The Dinosaur dinner": From *Jelly Belly* by Dennis Lee, copyright © 1983. Reprinted by permission of Macmillan of Canada, A Division of Canada Publishing Corporation.
- "Squirrels in my notebook": By Florence McNeil. From *Here Is a Poem*, published by the League of Canadian Poets, copyright © 1983. Reprinted by permission of the author.
- "Tinkering", "The sky is falling" and "Zeroing in": From *Oatmeal Mittens*, copyright © 1987 by Diane Dawber, Borealis Press. Reprinted by permission of the author.
- "Names don't always suit": By Nancy Prasad. From *Here Is a Poem*, published by the League of Canadian Poets, copyright © 1983. Reprinted by permission of the author.
- "Jeremy's house" and "Trip to the seashore": From *Auntie's Knitting a Baby*, copyright © 1984 by Lois Simmie. Reprinted by permission of Western Producer Prairie Books.
- "Thrum drew a small map": From *Gullband* by Susan Musgrave, copyright © 1974. Reprinted by permission of Douglas & McIntyre.
- "Waiting for the first drop" and "The Roundhouse": By Raymond Souster. From *Flight of the Roller Coaster*, copyright © 1985. Reprinted by permission of Oberon Press.
- "Recipe for Thanksgiving Day soup": By Dorothy Farmiloe. From *Here Is a Poem*, published by the League of Canadian Poets, copyright © 1983. Reprinted by permission of the author.
- "Nature": By Milton Acorn. From *I've Tasted My Blood*, copyright © 1969, McGraw-Hill Ryerson Limited. Reprinted by permission of the estate.
- "If you don't come": By Marguerite Mack. From *Alberta Poetry Yearbook*, 1975.
- "Fingerprint": By Harry Thurston. From *Barefaced Stone*. Fiddlehead Poetry Books, Fredericton, copyright © 1980. Reprinted by permission of the author.
- "Long, long ago": From *Bread, Wine and Salt*, copyright © 1967 by Alden Nowlan. Reprinted by permission of Irwin Publishing, Don Mills, Ontario.
- "Snake woman": From *Interlunar*, copyright © Margaret Atwood 1984. Reprinted by permission of Oxford University Press.
- "Together": By Carolyn Mamchur. Published by permission of the author.
- "The visitor": From *Scary Poems for Rotten Kids*, copyright © 1982 by sean o huigan. Reprinted by permission of Black Moss Press.
- "And even now": From *Collected Poems: The Two Seasons*, copyright © 1972 by Dorothy Livesay, published by McGraw-Hill Ryerson. Reprinted by permission of the author.
- "The royal visit" and "Windlady": From *Poems*, copyright © Canada 1972, by James Reaney, published by Press Porcépic. Reprinted by permission of the author.
- "Smart remark": From *Hey World, Here I Am*, by Jean Little, copyright © 1984. Reprinted by permission of Kids Can Press Ltd., Toronto, Canada.
- "My Moccasins have not walked": By Duke Redbird. From *Red on White: The Biography of Duke Redbird*, by Marty Dunn, copyright © 1971. Reprinted by permission of Stoddart Publishing, Don Mills, Ontario.
- "Here comes the witch": From *Don't Eat Spiders*, copyright © 1985 by Robert Heidbreder. Reprinted by permission of Oxford University Press Canada.
- "You better be ready": By John Lane, From *What Are Uncles For*, Harbour Publishing, copyright © 1985. Reprinted by permission of the author.
- "Licorice": By John Paul Duggan. From *Here Is a Poem*, published by the League of Canadian Poets, copyright © 1983. Reprinted by permission of the author.
- "Drums of my father": From *I Am an Indian*, copyright © 1969 by Shirley Daniels.
- "Too hot to sleep": From *Headwaters*, copyright © 1973 by Sid Marty. Reprinted by permission of the Canadian Publishers, McClelland and Stewart, Toronto.
- "Windigo spirit": By Ken Stange. From *Here Is a Poem*, published by the League of Canadian Poets, copyright © 1983. Reprinted by permission of the author.
- "Paul Bunyan": By Arthur S. Bourinot. From *Watcher of Men: Selected Poems 1947–1966*, Hurtig Publishers Ltd.